THE ITALIAN AMERICANS

THE ITALIAN AMERICANS

J. Philip di Franco

CHELSEA HOUSE PUBLISHERS
New York • Philadelphia

Cover Illustration: Paul Biniasz
Banner Design: Hrana L. Janto

5 7 9 8 6

Library of Congress Cataloging in Publication Data

di Franco, J. Philip.
    The Italian Americans.
    (The Peoples of North America)
    Bibliography: p.
    Includes index.
    Summary: Discusses the history, culture, and religion of the Italians, factors encouraging
their emigration, and their acceptance as an ethnic group in North America.

1. Italian Americans [1. Italian Americans]
I. Title. II. Series.
E184.I8D47 1987   973'.0451   86-31716

ISBN 0-87754-886-2
    0-7910-0268-3 (pbk.)

Contents

Nation of Nations

Senator Daniel Patrick Moynihan

The Constitution of the United States begins: "We the People of the United States . . ." Yet, as we know, the United States is not made up of a single group of people. It is made up of many peoples. Immigrants from Europe, Asia, Africa, South America, and Australia settled in North America seeking a new life filled with opportunities unavailable in their homeland. Coming from many nations, they forged one nation and made it their own. More than 100 years ago, Walt Whitman expressed this perception of America as a melting pot: "Here is not merely a nation, but a teeming Nation of nations."

It was the ingenuity and acts of courage of these immigrants, our ancestors, that shaped the North American way of life. Yet, we sometimes take their contributions for granted. This fine series, *The Peoples of North America*, examines the experiences and contributions of the immigrants and how these contributions determined the future of the United States and Canada.

The immigrants did not abandon their ethnic traditions when they reached the shores of North America. Each ethnic group had its own customs and traditions, and each brought different experiences, accomplishments, skills, values, styles of dress, and tastes in food that lingered long after its arrival. Yet this profusion of differences created a singularity, or bond, among the immigrants. The poet Robert Frost put it well: "The land was ours before we were the land's."

The United States and Canada are unique in this respect. Whereas religious and ethnic differences sparked wars throughout the rest of the world—from the 17th-century religious wars to the 19th-century nationalist movements in Europe to the near extermination of the Jews under Nazi Germany—*we* learned to respect each other's differences and to live as one.

And the differences were as varied as the millions of immigrants who sought a new life in North America. In a mass migration, some 12 million immigrants passed through the waiting rooms of New York's Ellis Island; thousands more came to the West Coast. At first, these immigrants were welcomed because labor was needed to meet the demands of the Industrial Age. Soon, however, the new immigrants faced the prejudice of earlier immigrants who saw them as a burden on the economy. Legislation was passed to limit immigration. The Chinese Exclusion Act of 1882 was among the first laws closing the doors to the promise of America. The Japanese were also effectively excluded by this law. In 1924, Congress established immigration quotas on a country-by-country basis.

Such prejudices might have erupted into war, as they did in Europe, but North Americans chose negotiation and compromise, instead. This determination to resolve differences peacefully has been the hallmark of the countries of North America.

The unique ability of Americans to live together as one people was seriously threatened by the issue of slavery. It was a symptom of a growing attitude of intolerance in the world. Thousands of English settlers had arrived in the colonies as indentured servants. These Englishmen agreed to work for a specified number of years on a farm or as a craftsman's apprentice in return for passage to America and room and board. When the first Africans arrived in the then-British colonies during the 17th century, some colonists thought that they should be treated as indentured servants, too. Eventually, the question of whether the Africans should be considered indentured, like the Englishmen, or slaves who could be owned for life, was considered in a Maryland court. The court's calamitous decree held that blacks were slaves bound to lifelong servitude, and so were their children. America went through a time of moral examination and civil war pitting brother against brother before it finally freed African slaves, as well as their descendants. The principle that all men are created equal had faced its greatest challenge and survived.

The court ruling that set blacks apart from other races fanned flames of discrimination that lasted long after slavery was abolished. The concept of racism had existed for centuries in countries throughout the world. When the Manchus conquered China in the 17th century, they decreed that Chinese and Manchus could not intermarry. To impress their superiority on the conquered Chinese, the Manchus ordered all Chinese men to wear their hair in a long braid called a queue.

By the 19th century, some intellectuals took up the banner of racism, citing Charles Darwin's work on the evolution of animals as proof of their position. Darwin's studies theorized that highly evolved animals were dominant over other animals. Some advocates of this theory applied it to humans, asserting that certain races were more highly evolved than others and thus were superior.

This philosophy served as the basis for a new discrimination, not only against certain races, but also against various ethnic groups. These ugly ideas were directed at black people and other victims as well. Asians faced harsh discrimination and were depicted by 19th-century newspaper cartoonists who chronicled public opinion as depraved, degenerate people, deficient in intelligence. When the Irish flooded American cities to escape the famine in

Ireland, the cartoonists caricatured the typical "Paddy" (a popular term for Irish immigrants) as an apelike creature with jutting jaw and sloping forehead.

By the 20th century, these concepts of racism and ethnic prejudice had developed into virulent theories of a Northern European master race. When Adolf Hitler came to power in Germany in 1933, he popularized the notion of Aryan supremacy. "Aryan," a term referring to the Indo-European races, was applied to so-called superior physical characteristics such as blond hair, blue eyes, and delicate facial features. Anyone with darker and heavier features was considered inferior. Buttressed by these theories, the German Nazi state from 1933 to 1945 set out to destroy European Jews, along with Gypsies and other groups considered inferior. It nearly succeeded. Millions of these people were killed.

How supremely important it is, then, that we have learned to live with one another, respecting differences while treasuring the things we share.

A relatively recent example of this nonviolent way of resolving differences is the solution the Canadians found to a conflict between two ethnic groups. The conflict arose in the mid-1960s between the peoples of French-speaking Quebec Province and those of the English-speaking provinces. Relations grew tense, then bitter, then violent. The Royal Commission on Bilingualism and Biculturalism was established to study the growing crisis and to propose measures to ease the tensions. As a result of the commission's recommendations, all official documents and statements from the national government's capital at Ottawa are now issued in both French and English, and bilingual education is encouraged.

The year 1980 marked a coming of age for the United States's ethnic heritage. For the first time, the U.S. Census asked people about their ethnic background. Americans chose from more than 100 groups, including French Basque, Spanish Basque, French Canadian, Afro-American, Peruvian, Armenian, Chinese, and Japanese, among others. The ethnic group with the largest response was English (49.6 million). More than 100 million Americans claimed ancestors from the British Isles, which includes Ireland, Wales, and Scotland. There were almost as many Germans (49.2 million) as English. The Irish-American population (40.2 million) was third, but the next largest ethnic group, the Afro-Americans, was a distant fourth (21 million). There was a sizable group of French ancestry (13 million), as well as of Italian (12 million). Poles, Dutch, Swedes, Norwegians, and Russians followed. These groups, and other smaller ones, represent the wondrous profusion of ethnic influences in North America.

Canada, too, has discovered the diversity of its population. Studies conducted during the French/English conflict determined that Canadians were descended from Ukrainians, Germans, Italians, Chinese, Japanese, native Indians, and Eskimos. Canada found it had no ethnic majority, although nearly half of its immigrant population came from the British Isles. Canada, like the United States, is a land of immigrants for whom mutual tolerance is a matter of reason as well as principle. Tolerance is a virtue that has brought North America peace.

The people of North America are the descendants of one of the greatest migrations in history. That migration is not over. Koreans, Vietnamese, Nicaraguans, and Cubans are heading for the shores of North America in large numbers. This mix of cultures shapes every aspect of our lives. To understand ourselves, we must know something about our ethnic ancestry, as well as about the ancestry of others, because in a sense, they are part of our history, too. Nothing so defines the North American nations as the motto on the Great Seal of the United States: *E Pluribus Unum*—Out of Many, One.

*New York City's Little Italy
preserved many features of
traditional village life.*

The Italian Influence Lives On

Few other ethnic groups have had as widespread an influence on America as the Italians have. Surely some of this influence is the result of the unusually large number of Italian immigrants who entered this country from the early 1800s to the early 1900s. Even today, that influence remains. The 1980 Census counted 12 million Americans of Italian ancestry and estimated that one in every 20 Americans is a descendent of Italian immigrants. With such a significant legacy, the Italian influence lives on.

The massive immigration lasted for more than 100 years, but it began to taper off in the 1930s, as fewer and fewer native-born Italians entered the country. Many Italians came to work temporarily in America, made their fortune, and then returned to Italy, but a significant number remained in America. The 1930 Census counted 1.8 million Italian-born residents in America. Of that number, three-fourths had emigrated from southern Italy—Na-

13

ples, Abruzzi, Molise, Puglia, Calabria, Campania—and the islands of Sardinia and Sicily.

This influx had an undeniable influence on America. Even today, the descendants of these immigrants celebrate the courage and the remembrances of their grandparents with visits to "Little Italies" and to Italy itself. They do not take lightly the importance of their ancestors' *paese* (village) connections. The vitality of that camaraderie is the most enduring quality of the Italian heritage. It allowed the Italian immigrants to overcome many obstacles and adjust to the many challenges that life offered them.

The majority of Italian immigrants left economically troubled Italy and arrived in America with less than $20 in their pockets. Many of them had been farmers in Italy, but fresh memories of the difficult

Italian Americans made America a premier wine-producing country.

Women flocked to the garment industry to boost family incomes.

and disappointing lives they had left behind made most of them reject their farming heritage. Avoiding anything that resembled farmwork, most Italian immigrants settled in America's cities. Still, some immigrants chose farming, and the ones who did made major contributions to American agriculture. For example, Italian-American farmers made America one of the finest wine-producing countries in the world.

Italian Americans have kept alive many of the customs and traditions of their heritage. Traditions from the village life that millions of Italian immigrants re-created in America's Little Italies are still visible in their descendants' religious festivals and family get-togethers. Yet, many Italian immigrants had to give up the customs that did not serve them well in America. For example, in the old country, women's roles revolved entirely around their home and children. The father was the undisputed head of the family, and no one made a decision without his approval. In America, Italian women, out of necessity, flooded the labor market. Giving up their traditional roles, these women entered the workplace, where they were encouraged to think independently and to Americanize quickly.

Education, which had been unavailable to peasants in Italy, pushed many second-generation Italian Americans to reject the ways

15

of their illiterate, old-world parents. In their struggle to adapt, some denied their Italian identity altogether and changed their names to more American-sounding ones. Today, these assimilationist attitudes have changed and many Italian Americans proudly retain their Italian names. One illustrious example is A. Bartlett Giamatti, formerly a literature scholar and the president of Yale University, and now the president of baseball's National League.

■ *This Veronese band was one of many that kept the Italian folk tradition alive in America.*

The Italian traditions, customs, and music that remain in America have been kept alive in family celebrations and public festivals, links to the life left behind in small villages from Naples to Sicily. Many Italian Americans still travel to Italy in search of their heritage. For the descendants of immigrants, this heritage is a reminder of their ancestors' accomplishments. Today these descendants can look back on a proud history of achievement in their adopted land.

The Florence cathedral is among the many architectural masterpieces built during the Renaissance.

Creativity in the Colonies

The American colonies had declared their independence from England nearly 100 years before the major Italian immigration began. But just before the colonies rebelled, some Italians began visiting the colonies in much the same way that an American student travels through Europe today—to experience the country and its people. While they weren't true immigrants, they influenced the colonists, who regarded them as worldly, learned men. These Italian visitors followed the tradition of the "Renaissance Man," who, like Leonardo da Vinci, studied philosophy, science, and the arts out of intellectual curiosity.

While residing in prerevolutionary America, Italians opened academies and boarding schools offering lessons in music, dancing, painting, writing, and even embroidery. They helped the colonists form their own artistic identity, one that eventually helped to separate them further from England.

☐ *New York City's National Theatre was built to satisfy colonial interest in the arts, awakened by Italians.*

The Italian influence helped diffuse the strict Puritan concept of the arts that had limited America's artistic development. Until this time, music in the Crown Colonies had been restricted to church hymns because the Puritans saw art as the work of the devil. After independence was declared, however, American artists became more expressive, and they looked to Italians for artistic inspiration. During this period, Thomas Jefferson invited Italian musicians to expand the United States Marine Corps band. Under the leadership of Gaetano Caruso, 14 Italians came to America and lifted the Marine Band from its fife-and-drum status to distinction.

Italian musicians also brought opera to America—perhaps their greatest contribution. Lorenzo de Ponte, who gained fame as Mozart's librettist, helped popularize opera in America when he opened the Italian Opera House in New York City in 1832. Although opera did not find a large audience until the mid-1800s, it now represents a significant part of America's musical scene.

A Philosopher Plants a Seed

Italian philosophers also influenced colonial America. Perhaps the best known of these was Filippo Mazzei, a physician from a small town near Florence. Mazzei impressed Benjamin Franklin with his philosophy and scientific knowledge. In 1771, George Washington, Thomas Jefferson, and other American planters commissioned Mazzei to conduct experiments to develop such crops as grapes and olives. With the help of a group of farm workers from Tuscany, Mazzei began his work on a property near Jefferson's plantation. Although he introduced many vegetables into American farming, the experiments were never completed because Mazzei's attention turned to the growing colonial rebellion against England.

Mazzei published his democratic theories in a series of articles under the pseudonym Furioso. His friend Thomas Jefferson trans-

■ *The philosophy of Filippo Mazzei inspired America's founding fathers.*

lated these articles from Italian to English for the *Virginia Gazette*. The words are strikingly similar to those which Jefferson wrote a few years later for the Constitution of the United States:

> All men are by nature equally free and independent. Such equality is necessary in order to create a free government. All men must be equal to each other in natural law. . . . A true Republican form of government cannot exist unless all men from the richest to the poorest are perfectly equal in their natural rights.

Art and Architecture

Fine art and architecture in America also owe much to these early Italian visitors. By the 19th century, their influence had lifted American art from its colonial "craft" status to a sophisticated level that

The Battle of La Hogue *was painted in 1778 by Benjamin West, an American who studied in Italy.*

attracted a cultivated audience and that enabled artists to broaden their skills and experiment with other forms.

Many of these artists set off for Europe to study. Benjamin West, the first American to win European recognition, studied in Italy from 1760 to 1763. He returned to America and taught such artists as Charles Willson Peale, Gilbert Stuart, and John Singleton Copley. As the Italian influence became prominent in American art, Italian artists flooded America.

The Italian artistic influence did not end with the revolutionary period. The United States government was the largest employer of Italian artists before the Civil War. Sculptor Giuseppe Ceracchi created official seals, insignias, and emblems for the young republic. He also sculpted busts of Washington, Jefferson, Franklin, and Adams. His bust of Hamilton is still considered one of the finest works of art created in pre-Civil War America.

A Land Divided

Many events led to the great migration from Italy during the 19th century. Natural disasters and an economy ruined by greedy landlords played a significant part. However, it was the struggle by other European rulers to control their Italian neighbors and the grip of the Roman Catholic church that did the most to sow the seeds of revolution in ravaged Italy. This revolution's failure to break the Italian peasants' dependence on the rich and powerful convinced millions of them to leave their native country.

From the earliest days of Western civilization, monarchs coveted Italy because it lay at the center of the Mediterranean Sea—the center of world commerce. Germanic tribes—Ostrogoths, Lombards, and Franks—invaded from the north. Muslims, Normans, Saracens, French, Spanish, Austrians, and Germans invaded the region south of Rome. But the Roman emperors held off these invasions so

25

successfully that eventually they controlled not only Italy but most of the known world as well. They ruled from 270 B.C. until 476 A.D. During their reign another force took shape. In Judea, a far-off territory of the Roman Empire, a carpenter preached the simple message that man should love his neighbor. In a world in which the rich and powerful held absolute control over the lives of the poor, the message of Jesus Christ shook the foundation of the Roman Empire.

When the followers of Jesus, called Christians, wanted to spread his teachings, they went to Rome—the crossroads of the known world. Rome eventually became a center of the Christian church. The head of this church, the pope, collected taxes and held the same authority as a monarch over the Italians. By the 19th century, the succession of popes had molded their authority into a powerful political alliance that ruled Europe.

The church's political alliances began in 800 A.D., when a pope crowned Charlemagne emperor of the Holy Roman Empire. After Charlemagne's death, this empire was divided among his grandsons into what is now France, Germany, and Italy.

However, Italy was not ruled by one monarch. Instead, the Italians split into two distinct peoples. The north developed into independent city-states, including Venice, Genoa, and Milan, ruled by powerful families. The south remained prey to invaders, and its people absorbed a mixture of cultures. Many of the northern city-states remained independent until the 17th century. Southern Italy, however, was controlled from 1522 until the late 1800s by the Spaniards.

During the long domination by the Spanish Hapsburgs, privileged landowners held the power of life and death over the southern peasants, or *contadini*. While the power of the landlords tied the contadini to the village and denied them any hope of economic advancement, the less restricted northern Italians became more worldly. The sharp distinctions between northern and southern Italians remained when they immigrated to America.

By the time American colonists fought for independence from England in the 1770s, Italy was separated into three parts. The pope

□ *Charlemagne, crowned emperor of the West in A.D. 800, solidified the political role of the Roman Catholic church.*

controlled the central part, called the Papal States, with the support of the French monarchy and its soldiers. Northern Italy's city-states had come under the power of the Austrian Empire. Southern Italy remained under Spanish rule. Despite this foreign domination, Italians never stopped fighting the invaders. Rebellions took place throughout the 1700s, and the leaders of those rebellions, often living in exile, helped inspire Americans to escape English rule.

Ironically, the American and French revolutions also helped the Italians win independence. France's politics became important to the Italians in 1796, when the French ruler Napoleon upset Italy's balance of power. Set on conquering Europe, Napoleon invaded Italy, took control, and drove the Austrians, the Spaniards, and the pope from power. But with Napoleon's defeat at Waterloo in 1815, control of Italy reverted to its previous status. Italy now consisted of the Kingdom of Sardinia (Piedmont, Sardinia, Savoy, and Genoa); the Kingdom of the Two Sicilies (including Naples and Sicily); the Papal States; 27

Tuscany, a series of smaller duchies in north central Italy; Lombardy; and Venice (controlled by the Austrians).

This power shift in Italy set the stage for revolution. After the Napoleonic Wars, the successful revolutions in America and France inspired the Italians to seek freedom from foreign control. When the French people overthrew Bourbon rule in 1831, the pope lost France's military support and the Italians revolted against the Papal States. A republic was proclaimed in Bologna, but Austria intervened and placed Bologna under military control. The Austrians also ruthlessly suppressed rebellions in Naples and Piedmont. Their repressive policies inflamed the Italians' already intense sentiments against foreign domination and gave rise to the Italian unification movement known as the *Risorgimento*.

Three men became heroes of this movement—Giuseppe Mazzini, Giuseppe Garibaldi, and Count Camillo Benso di Cavour. Americans followed their activities closely: Mazzini enjoyed the popular support of leading American intellectuals and liberals, and Garibaldi lived for a time in Staten Island, New York, as a celebrated exile.

Mazzini's leadership gave the movement momentum. His underground political fighters, called "Giovane Italia," or Young Italy, briefly drove the Austrians from Italy in 1831. They quickly recovered, however, and reestablished control of northern Italy. When Charles Albert (1798-1849) was proclaimed king of Sardinia in 1831, Mazzini tried to convince him to liberate Italy. Charles Albert refused. Although he later declared war on Austria and granted his people a constitution in 1848, his forces were crushed by Austria a year later.

After this defeat, Charles Albert abdicated in favor of his son, Victor Emmanuel II. In the meantime, Pope Pius IX began to feel threatened by the revolutionary movement. He had allowed some reforms in the Papal States, but now decided to rescind them. Before he could act, Garibaldi, an early follower of Mazzini, led an army into Rome in 1849 and proclaimed Italy a republic. Pope Pius IX left Rome, but the French soon regained power and reestablished papal authority.

Count Cavour used diplomacy and statesmanship instead of revolutionary force in his attempt to gain Italy's independence. The new

Giuseppe Garibaldi greets Italy's new king, Victor Emmanuel II, in 1861.

king of Sardinia-Piedmont, Victor Emmanuel II, named Cavour prime minister in 1852. Cavour formed alliances with Great Britain and France, sending the Sardinian army to fight by their side in the Crimean War. He expected this action would win France's help in ousting the Austrians from Italy. Soon after, in 1858, he negotiated an agreement with Napoleon III of France for a joint declaration of war against Austria.

But Napoleon reneged on the agreement and negotiated a treaty with the Austrians that ceded Lombardy, Sardinia, Savoy, and Nice to France. Although Cavour resigned as prime minister in protest, he soon returned to office and struck a new bargain with Napoleon. These new negotiations gained Romagna, Parma, Modena, and Tuscany for the kingdom of Sardinia-Piedmont.

In 1860, during Cavour's negotiations, Garibaldi raised an army and took control of Sicily. Victorious in Sicily, his troops then marched to Naples and won control of that territory. However, when Garibaldi began a march on Rome, Victor Emmanuel feared the French would intervene. He denounced Garibaldi and sent troops to stop him. Garibaldi surrendered. Cavour—using the pretext of preventing Garibaldi from taking Rome—sent Piedmont's army across the papal territory and claimed Sardinian authority over all of northern Italy except Venice.

The movement for Italy's unification seemed lost until 1866, when Italy and Prussia allied in the Seven Weeks' War to defeat Austria. This victory gave Italy control of Venice. The following year, Garibaldi led another army against the French-held Papal States, but the French forces again defeated it. Then, in 1870, Napoleon III suffered serious losses in the Franco-Prussian War, and the Papal States lost their French support. Italian troops took advantage of this opportunity and entered Rome on September 20, 1870. On July 2, 1871, Rome was proclaimed the capital of a united Italy. The Italians at last ruled their own country.

The newly unified Italy faced many problems. Years of separate loyalties had made the Italians a collection of different peoples and

In 1936 Victor Emmanuel III became emperor of a unified Italy.

opposing nobles. The pope's refusal to recognize the Italian state reinforced those separations. The impoverished southern peasants almost starved while greedy landlords drained the region of its scarce resources.

The profound gulf between the poverty-stricken south and the wealthier north widened. Italy seemed at war with itself, a condition that led Garibaldi to observe: "It has taken 100 years to unify Italy. It will take another 100 years to unify the Italian people." Unwilling to wait for Italy's economy to stabilize, millions of Italians abandoned their homeland and sought a new life in the New World.

I n Search of a Better Life

The first Italian immigrants to arrive in America came from northern Italy. A few had settled in America during the colonial period, but increasing numbers of northern Italian immigrants arrived after 1820. The discovery of gold in 1848 made life in America even more attractive, as did Italy's fight for independence in the 1870s.

Many Italian immigrants went first to several countries in South America, particularly Brazil and Argentina. However, a series of events turned the Italians toward North America. When a yellow fever epidemic in the late 1800s killed 9,000 Italian immigrants in Brazil, the Italian government temporarily banned immigration to that country. At the same time, a political crisis engulfed Argentina and Paraguay, dissuading immigrants from entering those countries.

Many of the northern Italian immigrants came to America from the rich farmland of Piedmont and

Liguria and settled in the fertile lands of California. Here, many of them opened successful wineries and citrus farms. By 1850, so many Italian immigrants had arrived in California that the king of Sardinia established an Italian consulate in San Francisco.

Many Italians became well known in California. Andrea Sbarbaro founded the Italian Swiss Colony winery in Sonoma in 1881. Marco Fontana founded the California Fruit Packing Corporation in 1889. His company, later called Del Monte, became the largest fruit and vegetable canning operation in the world.

The Mezzogiorno

Because northern Italian immigrant farmers were so successful in California and Florida, the United States began to reduce its imports of

Father and son haul grapes in California's wine region at the turn of the century.

fruit from the *mezzogiorno*, or southern Italy. Other factors further weakened southern Italy's economy. Plant lice destroyed thousands of acres of vineyards. Then, France placed a high tariff on Italian wine, making it too expensive for most Frenchmen to purchase. The southern Italian wineries of Puglia, Calabria, and Sicily faced disaster.

These economic setbacks, combined with a serious cholera epidemic that claimed 55,000 lives by 1887, left the southern Italian peasants barely able to survive. A severe crop failure in 1897 led to riots in Sicily, Puglia, and Calabria. Raids on bakeries and grain elevators followed in Naples. The contadini had had enough. They were ready to leave the villages where they had spent their entire lives.

For most contadini, the trip to America was their first outside the village where they had been born. In Italy their lives had revolved around a tightly knit, extended family and the *paese*, or village. They sought this same security in America, gathering in communities called Little Italies, where they were surrounded by *paesani* (people from the same village) who spoke the same dialect and practiced the same customs. In these neighborhoods, families and friends insulated themselves from the other Americans who were so different from them. As a result of this clannishness, the majority of southern Italians

35

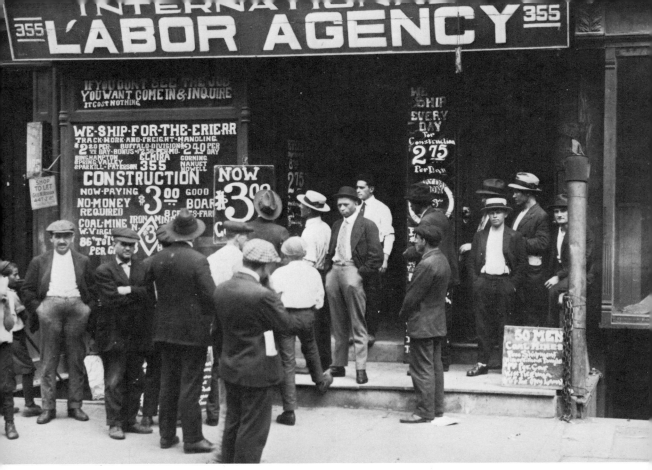

Labor agencies helped underskilled Italians find jobs in the New World.

remained in the cities, where housing was crowded but inexpensive. A large number settled in New York City, the port of entry for most Italians. By 1910, New York City's population included 340,000 Italians. The cities of Boston, Chicago, and Philadelphia each had Italian immigrant populations of about 45,000.

Although northern Italians had immigrated a generation before the contadini, they did not offer any help to the new immigrants from southern Italy. Ancient prejudices and different customs and dialects separated the two groups. Northerners saw themselves as more sophisticated than the southerners and tried to avoid any connection with them. Southern Italians' physical features also set them apart from other Italians. Many northern Italians were fair skinned, with Germanic features, whereas most southern Italians were darker, reflecting their combined Spanish, Arab, Moorish, Greek, and French ancestry.

When they arrived in America, many Italians had trouble finding work, for they lacked appropriate skills and education. Italy's feudal system had kept the peasants bound to the land, and in an environment where all hands were needed to contribute to the family income, parents did not encourage the pursuit of an education. Formal schooling was thus available only to priests and landowners, and more than half the southern Italians who immigrated to America were illiterate.

While other ethnic groups saw education as a way out of the ghetto and into prosperity, the Italian contadini seemed unaware that education could help them open doors. This attitude changed somewhat in 1917, when a new law required immigrants to pass a literacy test in English. Although this law was apparently intended to limit Italian immigration, Italians quickly adapted and sought the education they needed to gain admittance.

Although a large majority—more than 75 percent—of the southern Italians who emigrated by 1910 had been farm workers in Italy, most sought other occupations in America. For many, farm life represented the oppressive life they had fled. The majority of the newcomers settled in cities throughout New York, Pennsylvania, and New Jersey, where they replaced Irish immigrants in unskilled jobs with construction and railroad companies. Some followed the Jewish immigrants into the garment industry, while others sold vegetables

In New York City, Italian immigrants often became street laborers.

and fruits from pushcarts. Those who could afford businesses of their own opened small stores.

Italian women entered the New York garment industry in large numbers and still make up a large percentage of that work force. Italian men worked in the stockyards of Chicago and in the silk and textile factories of New England. They worked in the mines in Illinois and West Virginia and in the steel mills of Michigan and Pennsylvania. In San Francisco, Italian Americans created a lucrative fishing trade at Fisherman's Wharf.

Concerned about the fate of thousands of southern Italians congregating in the New York ghettos, a prominent Italian-American newspaper publisher, Generoso Pope, believed he had an answer. Along with Charles Landis, a wealthy philanthropist, Pope arranged low-interest loans to allow the southern Italian immigrants to buy farmland in New Jersey. As a result, Vineland, New Jersey, became the largest Italian community outside of Italy by the 1880s. Even today, the descendants of these immigrant farmers make up a large percentage of the Vineland farm community.

Despite their initial reluctance to resume farming, Italian farmers prospered throughout America. They transformed the swampland of western New York's Hudson River Valley into successful vineyards and raised cotton, sugar cane, and rice in the South. They planted successful apple and peach orchards in Arkansas and opened truck farms near metropolitan areas in Texas and Wisconsin.

Their limited education restricted most contadini to unskilled labor. Most Italian immigrants on the East Coast found work through Italian contract agents called *padroni*. In 1897, padroni controlled nearly two-thirds of New York's Italian labor force, especially in the construction trades. At the turn of the century, three-quarters of New York City's construction laborers were Italian. They made up nearly the entire labor force responsible for building the New York City subway system and manned most of the sand and gravel mines that provided the mortar for that extensive project. Italian laborers also built the Belmont Race Track.

■ *New Jersey cranberry pickers toil under the padrone's watchful eye during the Great Depression.*

The padroni system did not last long. As soon as the Italians could find work themselves, they turned away from the padroni. They preferred working independently and were reluctant to join labor unions. Still, when labor conditions became unbearable, they went on strike. During construction of the New York City subway, Italian workers struck several times and won demands for shorter hours and better pay. In Massachusetts, Italian textile workers waged a long, bloody strike for better pay.

The clannishness of the East Coast's Little Italy was less evident among the Italians who settled on the West Coast. These immigrants, who had arrived with enough money to travel across the country and to buy land, found that their paesano contacts were not extensive enough to meet the needs of their growing businesses in California. Amadeo Peter Giannini (1870–1949), a second-generation Italian American born in San Jose, helped these immigrants expand their limited business contacts by opening a bank for Italians. Other bank officials discriminated against Italian immigrants and often refused

them loans. But Giannini's Bank of Italy, which opened in San Francisco's Italian quarter in 1904, offered Italian-speaking tellers and free help in preparing naturalization papers. Giannini's Bank of Italy became one of the largest banks in the world—The Bank of America.

Despite the obstacles they faced, the Italian immigrants gained a reputation for good business sense, and a few achieved rags-to-riches success. One Italian immigrant, Amadeo Obici, had arrived in America at the age of 12. When he was 17, Obici operated his own fruit stand, specializing in the sale of roasted peanuts. Eventually, Obici's fruit stand business grew into the Planter's Peanut Company.

The peak years of the Italian immigration were 1900 to 1914. During those few years, more than 2 million Italians immigrated to America. The government of Italy encouraged emigration as a means of lessening the strain on its own economy. To improve its image

In the early 20th century, the international union movement protested poor working conditions.

☐ *This Italian-American storefront advertises a diversity of commercial services.*

overseas, the Italian government established passport requirements for emigrants in 1901. (Before this date, Italians had been permitted to leave without any special papers or permission.) It imposed a tax on prospective emigrants and denied a passport to anyone convicted of a crime. It also created the General Emigration Office to oversee all facets of emigration. The efforts of the Italian government paid off—Italian immigrants had the lowest rate of rejection of any ethnic group seeking entrance into the United States.

By the 1920s, many Americans had become disgruntled by the mass influx of foreigners and believed immigration should be limited. In 1921, and again in 1924, laws were passed that set quotas or limits on immigration. These quotas were based on the number of immigrants from each ethnic group that were currently living in America.

Surprisingly, this effort to restrict immigration actually benefited the Italians. So many of them had already immigrated that the Italian quota was high. Also, the quota did not restrict the immigration of spouses and children of United States citizens, so many Italian men became citizens to allow their families to immigrate more easily. As a result, Italians were able to immigrate at a rate three times the yearly quota.

The new life in America did not please all of the southern Italian peasants. Nearly half of the more than 4.5 million Italians who immigrated to the United States between 1876 and 1924 returned to Italy. However, the relative wealth of these returning emigrants continued to encourage emigration.

41

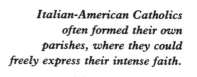

*Italian-American Catholics
often formed their own
parishes, where they could
freely express their intense faith.*

I talian Catholics in America

Other Catholics had immigrated to the United States before the Italians, but the way Italians expressed their faith set them apart from other Catholic immigrants. The southern Italian peasants who immigrated to America, primarily between 1900 and 1914, considered their version of Catholicism to be separate from the church hierarchy.

These peasants saw the Roman Catholic church as a political rather than a religious entity and viewed their religious practices as separate from the political affiliations of the Roman Catholic leaders. As a result, many other ethnic groups questioned the Italians' loyalty to the church because of their refusal to embrace the political leanings of the Catholic leaders.

These suspicions did not develop overnight but had been building for many centuries. In 1054, a dispute over a theological question split the Christian church into the Roman Catholic church and

43

 *Michelangelo's
sculpture of
Moses is a
triumph of
Renaissance
religious art.*

the Greek Orthodox church, creating two separate church hierarchies—one in Rome and the other in Greece. Two different civiliza-
tions evolved around these hierarchies. Later, disagreements between
the popes and other European political leaders created the Protestant
churches and led to battles between Catholics and Protestants in much
of Europe.

   During the Middle Ages, the popes took advantage of their political authority and the wealth it brought them to rebuild Rome,
which had fallen into decline after the split in 1054 that had divided
the church as well as the Roman Empire. During the period of artistic
renewal called the Renaissance, the popes and wealthy noble families,
such as the Medicis, sponsored artists and artisans throughout the
world. Once again, Rome became the center of commerce as well as
the center of Christianity. In addition, the papacy virtually controlled
artistic commissions and the content of all artistic projects. So, as
interest in Greek and Roman art increased, the power of the papacy

strengthened.

Eventually, the Roman Catholic popes ruled the area surrounding Rome, called the Papal States. Until the newly unified nation of Italy took away most of its property in 1873, the church was the largest single landowner in Italy. Because of the political power of the church hierarchy, Italian peasants regarded parish priests as noblemen who often sided with the rich landowners. As a result of these factors, the Italians' attitude toward the church as an institution was sometimes distrustful and anticlerical. Italian Catholics put more faith in the power of individual saints than in the clergy, whom they saw as agents of the rich and cruel landowners.

Because the southern Italians' heritage developed from many different cultures, Catholicism became a mix of ancient values, concepts, and symbols. Italian Catholicism developed into a unique philosophy that helped the Italian peasants cope with life's problems. They prayed to the saints for help with these problems and found escape by celebrating their faith with festive parades, in which they carried statues pinned with money through the streets while musicians played and vendors sold Italian food. These jubilant *festas* were held on certain holy days and the feast days of saints.

The San Genaro Festival is an annual highlight of New York City street life.

The Church's Role

When Italians arrived in America in the late 1880s, the Catholic clergy was, like its congregations, predominantly Irish. The Irish thought the flamboyant Italian religious customs attracted too much attention and opened Catholics to ridicule. Tensions grew, and many priests prohibited Italians from attending regular church services. The Irish priests pressured the Italians to abandon public shows of religious fervor and discouraged the mysticism of Italian Catholicism. During this period, the Italian immigrants often kept their children away from the Catholic schools because the clergy encouraged them to give up Italian traditions and customs.

The Italian immigrants responded to this attitude by pressuring the church to establish separate Italian parishes. The bishops at first refused but finally allowed national parishes with no geographic or neighborhood boundaries, such as Saint Anthony of Padua in New York City. Italian immigrants joined together to create these parishes, raising money and donating labor to build churches throughout America.

Despite their reluctant welcome into the American Catholic church, the Italian immigrants held firmly to their beliefs. They continued their customs, traditions, and rituals because they were a focal point of family life. Their religion set the tone for numerous family experiences—baptisms, first communions, confirmations, weddings,

■ *Many Italian-American families solemnly celebrate First Communion.*

46

(continued on page 55)

A Cultural Tapestry

More than two centuries after the philosophical ideas of Filippo Mazzei nourished America's founding fathers, Italian culture continues to influence the New World. Our architecture, much of it designed by Italians, pays homage to Renaissance models; Italian-American neighborhoods are vibrant centers in many cities; and our spiritual horizons have been expanded by the joyous festivity of Italian saints' days. A recent development—the emergence of prominent Italian-American politicians—testifies to this community's gift for weaving the old and the new into a rich and vivid tapestry.

The elegant symmetry of Italian art and architecture is shown above by Titian's The Concert *(c. 1515); in the facing portrait by Bronzino (c. 1545); and in Monticello, the Virginia mansion designed by Thomas Jefferson in 1770.*

49

Modern-day politics has been changed by three New York Italian Americans: Fiorello La Guardia, caricatured here as Napoleon; Geraldine Ferraro, who made history in the 1984 presidential race; and Mario Cuomo, elected governor in 1982.

51

Italian-Americans have enriched street life not only in New York City (below), but also in Wilmington, Delaware, whose massive St. Anthony of Padua Festival (pictured aerially) features vendors garbed in Old World costumes.

Roman Catholicism includes large-scale public displays, as demonstrated by the grand cathedrals where Italian Americans often worship and by outdoor processions honoring holy figures, such as St. Rocco, the patron saint of the afflicted.

(continued from page 46)

funerals, feast days, and even Sunday after-mass dinners. And although many second-generation Italian Americans married outside their ethnic group, they usually married other Catholics.

While Italians were finding little acceptance from the Catholic clergy, Protestant ministers stepped in to meet the spiritual and physical needs of the immigrants. For example, during the early part of the 20th century, the Protestant evangelical movement opened soup kitchens and recreation and education centers in Italian neighborhoods. The Protestant churches' involvement with the Italian Catholics finally spurred the Catholic church to begin helping Italian immigrants. In 1891, the Irish archbishop Michael Corrigan organized the Society of Saint Raphael to aid Italian immigrants and also established a temporary shelter in New York City for women and children. The Catholic clergy began to involve Italian Americans in activities associated with holy days and feast days of saints, as well as social organizations.

Eventually, the church sent priests and nuns who spoke both English and Italian to teach in America, and Italian immigrants began sending their children to the Catholic schools. To prepare priests for Italian-American parishes, Pope Leo XIII established the Apostolic College of Priests in Piacenza, Italy, in 1887. Two years later, he sent Mother Frances Xavier Cabrini with her Congregation of Missionary Sisters of the Sacred Heart to America. Her order established or-

In 1946 Mother Cabrini became the first U.S. citizen to be canonized by the Roman Catholic church.

55

phanages, hospitals, and schools for the Italian immigrants. Mother Cabrini, who became a naturalized citizen, was later named America's first saint by the Catholic church.

During this period, the Protestant missionaries continued to have an effect on the Italian population. By 1910, more than 300 Protestant missionaries were working full-time in Italian-American communities. Help from the Protestant clergy combined with the prevailing anti-Catholic sentiment to create a fervor for conversion: by 1916, about 50,000 Italians had joined American Protestant churches. Many saw it as a way to become more American.

Family Life

Life for second-generation Italian Americans was much different than it had been for their immigrant parents. The first generation saw American customs, such as unchaperoned dates and marriages with-

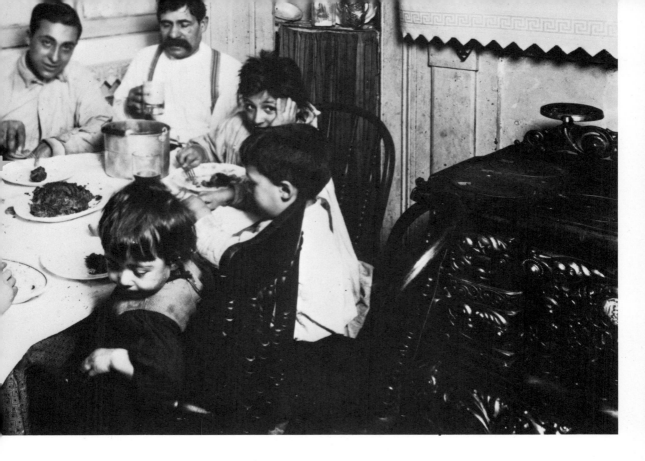

out parental consent, as destructive and dangerous. Thinking of themselves as Americans, their children were embarrassed by such old-fashioned customs.

Economic need altered the traditional Italian family structure. When America's economy plummeted in 1929, Italian-American family life began to change. In Italy, the father was the unquestioned head of the household, and the mother's duties tied her to home and children. In America, however, the Great Depression forced wives and daughters to seek work outside the home. They did so with little, if any, hesitation. Their work brought them into contact with other ethnic groups and pressured them to give up even more Italian customs. Although eager to embrace and be identified with American society, members of the second generation found it difficult to completely ignore their Italian heritage. In an effort to escape its hold, many Italian Americans moved away from Little Italy when they grew up, changed their names, and married non-Italians.

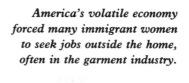

Overcoming the Obstacles

By the early 1900s, old-stock American ethnic groups blamed immigrants for the economic instability America was experiencing as it leaped from a rural nation to a highly industrialized country. To escape such blame, children of turn-of-the-century European immigrants abandoned their parents' native language and customs. However, second-generation Italian Americans had to overcome more than the usual ethnic stereotypes to become "American." Ironically, many of their troubles came from fellow Italians.

As the resentment toward foreigners intensified in the 1920s, northern Italians distanced themselves from the more recent arrivals. The large influx of southern Italians made them highly visible and a target of hostility in a country prejudiced against immigrants. Because they had little contact with Italian immigrants, non-Italians made assumptions about them based only on glimpses into the

59

ghettos. Many of these immigrants, single men who hoped to return to Italy, were viewed as "birds of passage"—temporary visitors who had no interest in contributing to America. In addition, the working-class immigrants did not fit the concept that many Americans had of the artistic, refined, Italian Renaissance man.

During this period, the sale of alcoholic beverages was banned. Some people—particularly the hard-pressed immigrants—saw this Prohibition Era as an opportunity to make quick profits from the illegal sale of liquor.

The Mafia Image Is Cast

When the press began to portray many Italians as being connected with the *mafia* (an Italian secret society), the stereotype of the gangster

Francis Ford Coppola's film **The Godfather** *caused a furor in 1972 because it perpetuated the negative image of Italians as gangsters.*

was cast. However, long before the Italians arrived in America, secret societies had existed in Italy. In the 1700s, the Spaniards ruled southern Italy, and they mistreated the Italian people. Because of abuses and betrayals suffered at the hands of these invaders, Italians were suspicious of all law enforcement authorities and viewed them as allies of the foreign landowners. In an effort to retaliate against such cruelty, some Italians formed secret organizations in which men allegedly swore to answer injustice or dishonor to their family by taking the law into their own hands.

In the 19th century, many powerful landowners in southern Italy went to the northern Italian cities in search of better business prospects. When they did, they sometimes left the management of their properties in the hands of the mafia. With such power, the mafia's members, or *mafiosi*, themselves became cruel tyrants, demanding loyalty from the peasants and taking control of southern Italy's economy.

Many members of these societies immigrated to the United States during the 1920s, leaving Italy because the Italian government began to prosecute mafia members. In America, the Italian immigrants' suspicion of the law, which represented tyranny in Italy, added to the mafia's strength.

The Italian-American Image

The movies sometimes contributed to the Italian Americans' negative image, because gangsters were commonly portrayed as being Italian. Audiences found the car chases and gunfire in these films visually dramatic; therefore, many gangster movies were made. This Hollywood tradition inadvertently perpetuated the stereotype of Italians as gangsters for decades.

Anti-Italian resentments in America lessened somewhat when Italy fought valiantly with the Allies in World War I. Italy had declared its neutrality at the onset of the war, but by 1916, it had declared war on Austria and Germany. When the Austrians broke through the

Italian line in October 1918, the Allies came to Italy's defense. Still, Italy suffered great losses: its World War I casualties numbered more than 450,000. After World War I, America's acceptance of Italian immigrants improved slowly, in part because of the Italian Americans' participation in the war.

Political Identity

Although most Italians in America had not, so far, involved themselves in American politics, many had a strong sympathy for political movements in Europe. After World War I, a new political philosophy swept the world, one that called for the abolition of all government. It was called anarchism. The Russian Revolution inspired it and political oppression in Europe strengthened it. Italian-American involvement in this movement first surfaced when the Italian king Humbert I was assassinated on July 29, 1900. The assassin was Gaetano Bresci, a silk worker in Paterson, New Jersey, who had returned to Italy. Bresci's connection with the growing Anarchist movement focused worldwide attention on this new philosophy and the involvement of Italian Americans in politics.

A fanatic opposition to the Italian Americans who supported another political movement, socialism—which called for collective or governmental control of the economy—erupted in the 1920s with the Sacco and Vanzetti trial. Two Italian-American men who were known supporters of the Socialist movement were arrested for a crime that had been committed nearly a month earlier. On April 15, 1920, robbers had stolen $15,000 in cash and killed the paymaster and a guard at a shoe manufacturing company in a small community 12 miles (19 kilometers) south of Boston.

Although there was little evidence against them, Nicola Sacco and Bartolomeo Vanzetti were arrested while riding a streetcar. The hysteria surrounding their trial attracted worldwide attention and for some people still symbolizes legal injustice based on prejudice. The Italian government appealed for justice, but the two men were con-

🔲 *Italian Americans Nicola Sacco and Bartolomeo Vanzetti were tried and executed for murder despite the lack of evidence against them.*

victed and sentenced to death. After 7 years and numerous appeals, Sacco and Vanzetti were put to death on August 23, 1927. The prosecution's argument that these men were capable of such a crime because they were Italian provoked pro-Italian demonstrations throughout the world.

Vanzetti's final statement to the court addressed the injustice he and many others felt:

> I am suffering because I was a radical and indeed I am a radical.
> I have suffered because I was an Italian and indeed I am an Italian.

Support for Fascism

Hostility against Italian Americans intensified during the 1920s when many of them became involved in Benito Mussolini's Fascist reform

63

Many Italian Americans supported Fascist leader Benito Mussolini in the 1930s.

Roman crowds cheer the victorious end of the war against Ethiopia in 1935.

movement in Italy. The constant political maneuverings at the turn of the century had left Italy in a state of unrest that fostered the growth of the Fascists, a new political party that sought to install a dictatorial government that would regulate all economic and social policy. Under Mussolini, the Fascists fought against the Communists, who were themselves calling for government reform, in Rome, Bologna, Genoa, Trieste, Alessandria, and Parma. In October 1922 the black-shirted Fascist army marched on Rome and demanded control

of the Italian government. Their revolt met with little resistance; Italian cabinet minister Luigi Facta resigned, and the king gave Mussolini the authority to form a new government.

Mussolini instilled such national pride in Italy that many Italian Americans praised him and embraced his political doctrine. They were disappointed when America gave token aid to Italy's archenemy, Austria, because Mussolini's wartime actions had placed him on the side of the Allies.

However, Mussolini and the Fascist movement soon became so extreme that Italian Americans withdrew their support. The Fascists began suppressing all other political parties in the country. Later, the Lateran Treaty in 1929 dissolved the civil power of the popes.

By 1939, Mussolini had become obsessed with controlling all of Italy and accelerated his drive for power. He replaced the Chamber of Deputies, which represented several political parties, with the Chamber of Fasci and Corporations. This move completely eliminated all official opposition.

Mussolini then plunged his nation into war. He annexed Ethiopia in May 1936 and proclaimed Victor Emmanuel III, the king of Sardinia, emperor of a united Italy. In the same year, he sent troops to aid General Francisco Franco in the Spanish civil war (1936–1939), in which the Italian army suffered heavy casualties: about 4,000 Italians were killed and more than 15,000 were wounded. In 1939, Mussolini shocked supporters around the world by forming an alliance with German chancellor Adolf Hitler.

Then, World War II erupted. Italy aligned with Germany against the United States, shocking Italian Americans who had supported Mussolini and destroying any Italian-American support for the Italian government.

Updating the Image

More than a million Italian Americans fought valiantly for the United States in World War II. Thirteen received the Congressional Medal of Honor and ten received the Navy Cross. The G.I. Bill allowed many Italian Americans to pursue higher education and enabled them to secure better positions in industry and the arts.

By the 1940s, the Italian-American image was enhanced, even glamorized, by a real-life hero, New York Yankees baseball player Joe DiMaggio. Americans of all ethnic backgrounds cheered for the Yankee Clipper. After the war, operatic tenor Mario Lanza added another facet to this favorable image with his romantic singing roles in the movies. Frank Sinatra, the idol of thousands of swooning American teenagers in the 1940s, became a box-office success at the moviehouses.

The image of Italian Americans as gangsters was resurrected in the 1950s, however, when a popular television series, "The Untouch-

Most Italian Americans withdrew their support for Mussolini after he allied with Adolf Hitler in 1939.

ables," depicted government agents fighting Italian racketeers, week after week. Then, in 1969, Mario Puzo's novel *The Godfather* sparked mafia mania at the movies once again. But by the 1970s, television had begun to depict Italians on the right side of the law, in such shows as "Columbo" and "Baretta," and the movies offered *Serpico*,

 A flag-raising ceremony in New York City's Little Italy honors local men serving in World War II.

based on the real-life heroism of an Italian-American policeman. One of the most popular images of Italian Americans in the movies was that of Rocky Balboa, the character created by actor-director Sylvester Stallone. A prizefighter with a heart of gold, Rocky fought to uphold his own code of honor while honoring the integrity of others.

Italian-American Contributions

Since colonial times, Italians have helped to advance the quality of life in America. Even those who never became United States citizens made significant contributions. The opportunities the immigrants found and the sacrifices they made enabled their children to gain prominence. Today, many generations of Italian Americans continue to enrich and enliven the American experience.

Guglielmo Marconi (1874-1937), who was born in Bologna, Italy, refined the wireless telegraph—the forerunner of radio—in 1895, while working in America. He also developed the short wave transmitter, which allowed President Theodore Roosevelt to send a transatlantic message in 1903. Marconi received the Nobel Prize for physics in 1909 and returned to Italy in the 1920s. The company he formed in 1899 in New York, the Marconi Wireless Company of America, developed into the Radio Corporation of America (RCA).

71

When Enrico Fermi (1901-1954) immigrated to America in 1938, he attracted international attention. Born in Rome, Fermi became a professor of theoretical physics at the University of Rome, where he developed a statistical theory that explained how electrons behaved. In 1938, Fermi won the Nobel Prize for his work with artificial radioactivity. But when he prepared to travel to Sweden to accept the award, Italy's Fascist government tried to prevent him and his wife from leaving the country. He finally obtained passports, but he angered Mussolini by refusing to give the Fascist salute during the Nobel Prize ceremonies. While in Sweden, he decided to immigrate to the United States.

In December 1942 Fermi created the first controlled nuclear fission chain reaction. He later became a consultant on the "Manhattan

Project," which developed the first atomic bomb, and was director of the new Institute of Nuclear Studies at the University of Chicago from 1946 until his death.

Arts and Entertainment

Arturo Toscanini (1867-1957), born in Parma, Italy, conducted many memorable performances as orchestra director of the New York Metropolitan Opera Company. He held that position from 1909 until 1915, when he returned to Italy. After several years as orchestra director at Italy's leading opera house, La Scala, he returned to the Met. His orchestral performances were so popular that the National Broadcasting Company (NBC) created an orchestra for him in 1937.

■ *Tenor Enrico Caruso, in costume here for* **The Masked Ball,** *delighted Metropolitan Opera audiences in New York City.*

This orchestra's popular radio broadcasts introduced classical music to audiences across America.

Noted for conducting entire scores from memory, Toscanini insisted on performing works according to the composer's original intention. His style set a new standard for orchestra directors, eliminating the liberal interpretations of classical music that had been popular with his predecessors.

Italian opera singers found a special place of honor in America. Enrico Caruso (1873-1921) became a worldwide success with his role of Loris in *Fedora*, an opera by Umberto Giordano, in 1898. Caruso made his American debut at the Metropolitan Opera in 1903. The American audience was enthralled by his powerful, clear voice. A perfectionist as a performer, he was a favorite at the Met for nearly 18 years and hailed as the greatest tenor in the world. He had an extensive repertoire but is especially remembered for his role of Canio in *I Pagliacci*, by Ruggiero Leoncavallo.

Another great operatic tenor was the Italian-American singer Mario Lanza (1921-1959), who was born in Philadelphia. Lanza attained success through concert tours, radio performances, opera recordings, and movies. He was the first vocalist to receive a gold record, which he earned for his recording of "Be My Love." Lanza, a major screen star, portrayed Enrico Caruso in the movie *The Great Caruso*. His other films include *That Midnight Kiss*, *Toast of New Orleans*, *Because You're Mine*, and *Serenade*.

America's entertainment industry attracted many Italian Americans. Hollywood film director Frank Capra was born on May 18, 1897, in Palermo, Sicily. He immigrated to America with his family when he was six years old and settled in Los Angeles. Capra began his Hollywood career as a writer for the Mack Sennet Studios, creator of the "Our Gang" comedies. At Columbia Pictures, Capra gained a reputation for directing sophisticated comedies with happy endings and social overtones.

Capra won Academy Awards for his direction of Clark Gable and Claudette Colbert in *It Happened One Night*, which won four Oscars, and for *Mr. Deeds Goes to Town* and *You Can't Take It With You*. But perhaps his most enduring movies are *Lost Horizon*, *Mr. Smith Goes to Washington*, and *It's a Wonderful Life*. Capra retired to Palm Springs, California, in 1971, where he wrote his autobiography, *The Name Above the Title*.

Frank Sinatra became teenage America's first idol when his soft, "crooning" singing style left 1940s teenagers breathless. The son of Sicilian immigrants, he was born in a rough Italian neighborhood in Hoboken, New Jersey, on December 12, 1917. His father, Martin, worked as a boilermaker and gained some fame as a professional boxer under the name Marty O'Brien.

Sinatra performed with both the Harry James Orchestra and the Tommy Dorsey Orchestra. He recorded his first big hit, "I'll Never

Although Frank Sinatra has been the focus of controversy, his gifts as a vocalist are beyond dispute.

Smile Again," in 1940. Later, he acted and sang in Hollywood films, including *Anchors Aweigh*, *On the Town*, and *Till the Clouds Roll By*. He won critical acclaim for his dramatic performances in *From Here to Eternity*, *The Manchurian Candidate*, and *The Detective*.

Anne Bancroft, the award-winning actress, was born Anne Marie Italiano on September 17, 1931, in the Bronx, New York. The daughter of Italian immigrants, Bancroft studied acting in New York and then began her career in Hollywood films. After six years, she became dissatisfied with her lack of success and returned to New York. The response to her Broadway performance in *Two for the Seesaw* was outstanding, and her role in *The Miracle Worker* (1962) won her several dramatic awards, including an Oscar. Bancroft co-starred in several movies directed by her husband, comic Mel Brooks, including *Silent Movie* and *To Be or Not To Be*.

Politics

Fiorello La Guardia (1882-1947), who served three terms as mayor of New York City, was born of Italian-immigrant parents in New York City's Greenwich Village. Before entering politics, La Guardia had worked as a diplomat, an interpreter at Ellis Island, and a pilot during World War I. After earning a law degree, he began a private law practice, primarily assisting immigrants. He was appointed a deputy attorney general in New York in 1914 and later was elected president of the New York City Board of Aldermen, the first Italian American to successfully challenge the Irish dominance of New York City politics.

La Guardia was a colorful figure with a reputation as a progressive, honest politician and was affectionately known as the Little Flower, the English translation of his first name. He served as mayor of New York City from 1933 until his voluntary retirement in 1945 and was elected to Congress twice. While mayor, La Guardia conducted a popular weekly radio show. He is fondly remembered for reading the daily comic strips over the radio for the children of New

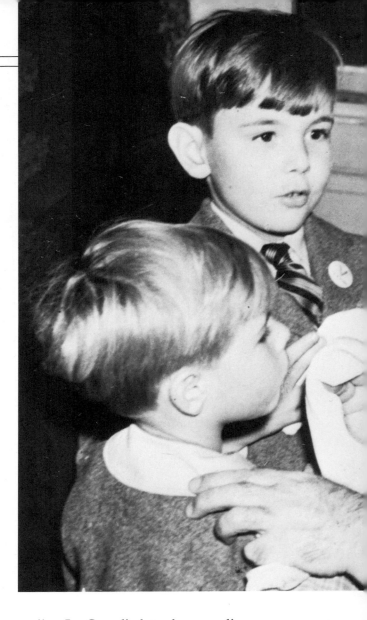

York during a long newspaper strike. La Guardia later became director of the United Nations Relief and Rehabilitation Administration.

Geraldine Ferraro, the first American woman nominated for vice-president by a major party, ran with Walter Mondale on the Democratic ticket against President Ronald Reagan in 1984. Born on August 26, 1935, in Newburgh, New York, where her immigrant parents owned a restaurant and a five-and-dime store, Ferraro graduated from Manhattan's Marymount College in 1956 and then attended night

classes at Fordham University Law School. She became a lawyer and was appointed an assistant district attorney in New York. Elected to Congress in 1978, Ferraro proved herself a shrewd and accomplished politician. She wrote her autobiography, *Ferraro: My Story*, after losing the race for vice-president and continues to play a key role in national politics.

Mario Cuomo, governor of New York State, was born on June 15, 1932, in the borough of Queens in New York City. His parents

■ *Political forecasters predict that Mario Cuomo will continue to play a major role in national politics.*

immigrated to America from Salerno, Italy, in the 1920s. He worked as an attorney for nearly two decades before New York Governor Hugh Carey appointed him secretary of state in 1975. Cuomo lost a New York mayoral race but was elected lieutenant governor on a ticket with Carey in 1978. In 1982, Cuomo was elected governor. He gained national attention with his stirring address at the 1984 Democratic party convention nominating Geraldine Ferraro for vice-president.

Antonin Scalia, the first Italian American appointed to the Supreme Court, was born on March 11, 1936, in Trenton, New Jersey, the son of immigrants. Scalia graduated at the top of his class from Georgetown University and served as a law review editor while attending Harvard Law School. Later, he was appointed to head President Gerald Ford's office of legal counsel. Scalia taught at the University of Chicago for six years before President Reagan appointed him to the federal appellate court in the District of Columbia. In June 1986, he was nominated as a Supreme Court justice and in August of that year received the Senate's overwhelming approval.

Italian-American Heroes

Joe DiMaggio, one of baseball's greats, was born on November 25, 1914. From 1936 to 1951, DiMaggio led the New York Yankees to 10 World Championships, maintained a .325 lifetime batting average, and hit 361 home runs. He was voted Most Valuable Player in 1939, 1941, and 1947. These accomplishments earned him a permanent place in the National Baseball Hall of Fame in 1955. DiMaggio's marriage to actress Marilyn Monroe added to his celebrity status, although the marriage ended in divorce.

Lee Iacocca, president of the Chrysler Corporation, was born Lido Anthony Iacocca on October 15, 1924. The son of Italian immigrants, Iacocca grew up in Allentown, Pennsylvania, where he discovered an instinct for marketing while working at moviehouses his father owned. After the family business was lost during the Great

Depression, Iacocca studied engineering at Lehigh and Princeton universities. He took a job as a student engineer in 1946 at Ford Motor Company and worked his way up the corporate ladder. While at Ford, he designed the highly successful Mustang convertible. His achievement in making the Mustang a success helped him attain the position of Ford Motor's president in 1970. He successfully ran the company

■ *Joe DiMaggio's phenomenal achievements on the diamond made him a national hero.*

eight years but left after a 1978 dispute with Henry Ford.

After leaving Ford, Iacocca took over the financially troubled ysler Corporation and today is credited for its miraculous recov- His business success, combined with his role as chairman of the ue of Liberty–Ellis Island Centennial Commission, has made Ia- a an American folk hero.

*Three generations of Italian
Americans embody the
perseverance of Italian
immigrants in the United States.*

The Fabric of America

The Italian heritage has had a strong influence on the Italian-Americans' life-style. One of its strongest influences has been its cultural legacy. But perhaps a more important influence has been the Italians' sense of dignity and perseverence despite the difficulties they faced. The immigrants' story shines as an example of overcoming obstacles no matter what the odds.

The Italian immigrants cut a niche for themselves in the fabric of America. It was not easy, but they persevered. Their endurance enabled them to wait for the doors of opportunity to open, if not for them, then for their children. However, remnants of the prejudice the immigrants experienced linger in Hollywood's stereotypes of Italian gangsters and in persistent stories of organized crime connections.

As members of the younger generation adapted to their modern American world, many of their values changed. Religion—a traditional source of Italian-American strength—remained a mainstay, even when beliefs disagreed with the teachings of the Catholic church. But this enduring sense of spirituality has taken a different turn for later generations, many of whom reject the strict rules of Catholicism. This has led to a quiet rebellion against organized religion, similar perhaps to the earlier attitude of the southern Italian villagers.

The Italian immigrants' view of politics in America evolved in much the same way as their religion did. Believing that political office was only for the upper class, the Italian Americans entered politics later than other ethnic groups. But once they did, they exerted an important influence in politics. With Fiorello LaGuardia in the past and Mario Cuomo and Geraldine Ferraro in the foreground today, the tradition continues.

The Catholic church and its teachings have bolstered generations of Italian Americans.

Italian Americans gained influence in Philadelphia politics after the Second World War.

Millions of Italian immigrants sacrificed and sometimes barely survived to enable their children and grandchildren to take full advantage of the American Dream. Third- and fourth-generation Italian Americans are securely rooted in the American lifestyle. For them, participation in Italian traditions may be only a leisure activity. Yet, they honor the values of their grandparents. Those values—loyalty, hard work, and religious devotion—serve them well in the modern world.

Selected References

Alba, Richard. *Italian Americans: Into the Twilight of Ethnicity*. Englewood Cliffs, N.J.: Prentice-Hall, Inc., 1985.

Lopreato, Joseph. *Italian Americans*. Ethnic Groups in Comparative Perspective. New York: Random House, 1970.

Starr, Dennis. *The Italians of New Jersey: A Historical Introduction and Bibliography*. Newark: New Jersey Historical Society, 1985.

Tomasi, Lydio, ed. *Italian Americans: New Perspectives in Italian Immigration and Ethnicity*. New York: Center for Migration Studies of New York, Inc., 1985.

Index